LANGI___

TRAVEL GUIDE
2023

The Best Travel Budget and Ultimate Travel Companion for Family Vacation, Senior's Trip, Tourists, Students and Solo Travelers

LISA HANSON

Copyright © 2023, Lisa Hanson

TABLE OF CONTENTS

INTRODUCTION

CHAPTER ONE:

Introduction to Langkawi

- Discovering Langkawi
- Brief History of Langkawi
- Geography and Climate
- Getting to Langkawi
- Local Transportation

CHAPTER TWO:

Planning Your Trip

- Choosing the Best Time to Visit
- Setting Your Budget
- Accommodation Options
- Creating an Itinerary
- Travel Essentials and Packing Tips

CHAPTER THREE:

Exploring Langkawi's Neighborhoods

- **Pantai Cenang and the Beachfront**
- **Kuah Town and Shopping District**
- **Datai Bay and Luxury Resorts**
- **Telaga Harbor and the Marina**

CHAPTER FOUR:

Must-See Attractions

- **Langkawi Cable Car and Sky Bridge**
- **Langkawi Wildlife Park**
- **Tanjung Rhu Beach**
- **Langkawi Underwater World**
- **Langkawi Geopark**
- **Eagle Square (Dataran Lang)**

CHAPTER FIVE:

Experiencing Langkawi's Culture

- **Langkawi's Culinary Scene**
- **Traditional Malay Cuisine**

- Festivals and Events
- Traditional Arts and Crafts
- Local Markets and Souvenirs

CHAPTER SIX:

Outdoor Adventures and Recreation

- Beach Activities and Water Sports
- Trekking in Langkawi's Rainforests
- Island Hopping and Boat Tours
- Golfing in Langkawi
- Day Trips and Excursions

CHAPTER SEVEN:

Langkawi for Families, Seniors, and Solo Travelers

- Family-Friendly Activities
- Langkawi for Seniors
- Solo Travel Tips and Safety
- Meeting Locals and Making Friends

CHAPTER EIGHT:

Practical Information and Resources

- **Money and Currency**
- **Language and Communication**
- **Safety and Health Tips**
- **Sustainable Travel in Langkawi**
- **Useful Contacts and Emergency Numbers**

APPENDIX I:

Useful Travel Resources

- **Helpful Travel Apps**
- **Langkawi Travel Check**
- **Currency and Banking Information**

APPENDIX II:

Glossary of Malay Phrases

- **Basic Phrases for Travelers**
- **Ordering Food and Drinks**
- **Navigating Public Transportation**

APPENDIX III:

Maps of Langkawi

INTRODUCTION

Welcome, dear travelers, to the enchanting paradise known as Langkawi! As a witness to the bewitching beauty and captivating charm of this tropical haven, I am overjoyed to extend my warmest welcome and share with you the wonders that await in my "Langkawi Travel Guide 2023." Brace yourselves for an immersive journey into a realm where emerald waters kiss powder-white shores, ancient legends come to life, and every moment is a symphony of tropical delight.

Langkawi, a gem nestled in the Andaman Sea off the northwest coast of Malaysia, is a realm where nature weaves its magic with grace and grandeur. In this guide, I shall regale you with tales of sun-kissed beaches, lush rainforests teeming with life, and the vibrant local culture that beckons explorers from around the world.

As you turn the pages of this book, be prepared to embark on an odyssey that will take you through the very heart of Langkawi's wonders. Discover the secrets of the Seven Wells Waterfall, where legend mingles with reality, or immerse yourself in the mystical depths of the Langkawi Geopark, where ancient landscapes whisper tales of millennia past.

But Langkawi is more than just its natural splendor. It is a tapestry woven with the threads of history, culture, and gastronomy. Savor the flavors of mouthwatering Malaysian cuisine as you dine by the shores of Pantai Cenang, and delve into the rich heritage of this island as you explore the Mahsuri Tomb and the Al-Hana Mosque.

For the adventure-seekers among you, Langkawi offers an array of thrilling activities, from island hopping and snorkeling to jungle treks and even the exhilarating Langkawi Sky Bridge, offering panoramic vistas that will leave you breathless.

Throughout this guide, I shall be your trusted companion, sharing insider tips, hidden gems, and practical advice to make your Langkawi sojourn truly unforgettable. Whether you're a sun worshiper, a nature enthusiast, a history buff, or simply a curious wanderer, Langkawi has something to offer every soul.

So, flip through these pages, let your imagination take flight, and allow the allure of Langkawi to wash over you. With "Langkawi Travel Guide 2023" in your hands, your journey to this island paradise is about to begin – a journey filled with wonder, discovery, and boundless joy. Welcome to Langkawi – where dreams come true, and reality surpasses even the wildest of imaginations. Let the adventure begin!

CHAPTER ONE:
Introduction to Langkawi

Discovering Langkawi

Langkawi, a tropical paradise nestled in the emerald waters of the Andaman Sea, entices visitors from all over the world. Langkawi is a location that promises enchantment at every turn, thanks to its spectacular natural beauty, diversified ecosystems, and rich cultural legacy.

Imagine walking along gorgeous beaches with fluffy white sands and crystal-clear waters. Imagine vast jungles filled with exotic flora and animals, their canopies reverberating with the enchanting symphony of exotic birds. Consider towering limestone structures rising high from the soil, as well as inhabitants' warm, inviting smiles as they welcome you to their bustling communities. This is the essence of Langkawi, a place where nature and culture coexist in perfect harmony.

Brief History of Langkawi

To really appreciate Langkawi, one must dig into its fascinating history, which is steeped in folklore and sculpted by centuries of human impact. Langkawi's history, like its natural beauty, is braided with various strands.

The name "Langkawi" itself is thought to have originated from the Malay words "helang" (eagle) and "kawi" (reddish brown), inspired by the island's majestic eagle population and the reddish-brown tint of its geological formations.

Historical records suggest that Langkawi has been inhabited for thousands of years. Early settlers are believed to have been from the southern regions of Thailand, giving the island a rich cultural blend. The archipelago's strategic location along ancient trade routes made it a coveted prize for various empires and traders, including the Siamese, the Kedah Sultanate, and the British.

During the 19th century, Langkawi became a haven for pirates, further enhancing its mystique. One of the most famous legends associated with the island is that of Princess Mahsuri, a local maiden wrongfully accused of adultery and subsequently cursed the island for seven generations. Her tragic tale is woven into the fabric of Langkawi's identity, with the Mahsuri Tomb serving as a poignant reminder of her story.

The Malaysian government gave duty-free status to Langkawi in 1987, making it into a tourist magnet and contributing to its economic growth. The island's classification as a UNESCO-listed Langkawi Geopark in 2007 cemented its standing as a natural wonder of global significance.

Today, Langkawi continues to captivate visitors with its blend of natural beauty, cultural diversity, and a touch of mysticism. Its history is a testament to the resilience of its people and their ability to thrive in harmony with the environment.

Geography and Climate

Langkawi's geography is a testament to the awe-inspiring beauty of nature. This archipelago consists of 99 islands (104 at low tide) set against the backdrop of the azure Andaman Sea. The largest and most developed island is Pulau Langkawi, where the majority of tourist activities are centered. The islands are characterized by their diverse landscapes, which include lush rainforests, mangrove swamps, limestone hills, and idyllic beaches.

Langkawi's climate is tropical, delivering warm and humid weather all year. The island has two distinct seasons: the wet season, which lasts from April to October, and the dry season, which lasts from November to March. The wet season is characterized by heavy rain showers and high humidity, whereas the dry season is distinguished by pleasant weather with less rainfall and cooler temperatures. The dry season is the greatest time to visit Langkawi for outdoor activities and clear sky, however the island's natural beauty may be enjoyed all year.

Getting to Langkawi

Langkawi is easy to get to thanks to its well-connected transportation options:

- By Air: Langkawi International Airport (LGK) is the island's major gateway and a hub for domestic and international aircraft. It has direct flights to major Malaysian cities such as Kuala Lumpur, Penang, and Johor Bahru, as well as foreign destinations like Singapore and Bangkok.

- By Sea: If you prefer a more leisurely approach, Langkawi can also be reached by ferry from several ports on the mainland, including Kuala Kedah,

Kuala Perlis, and Penang. The ferry journey provides picturesque views of the Andaman Sea and the surrounding islands, making it a memorable experience in itself.

Local Transportation

Once you've set foot on Langkawi, getting around the island is a breeze, thanks to various transportation options:

- Car Rental: Renting a car is a popular choice for travelers who want the freedom to explore Langkawi at their own pace. Numerous rental agencies offer a range of vehicles, from compact cars to SUVs, ensuring you can comfortably traverse the island's diverse terrain.

- Motorcycle and Scooter Rentals: For a more adventurous and economical way to get around, consider renting a motorcycle or scooter. These two-wheeled options are perfect for navigating Langkawi's winding roads and accessing secluded spots.

- Taxi Services: Taxis are readily available on the island, making it convenient to move between attractions and destinations. Ensure that the meter is turned on or agree on a fare with the driver before starting your journey.

- Local Buses: Langkawi's public bus system offers an affordable mode of transportation, especially for budget-conscious travelers. Buses connect various parts of the island, although their schedules may be less frequent compared to larger cities.

- Bicycle Rentals: For eco-conscious travelers or those seeking a leisurely pace, renting a bicycle is an excellent way to explore Langkawi's quieter, more scenic routes. The island's relatively flat terrain makes it suitable for cycling.

Navigating Langkawi is part of the adventure, allowing you to uncover hidden gems, breathtaking viewpoints, and charming villages. Whether you prefer the convenience of a rental car, the wind in your hair on a scooter, or the simplicity of a bicycle, Langkawi's transportation options cater to every traveler's preferences.

CHAPTER TWO: Planning Your Trip

Careful planning before leaving on your Langkawi excursion can make all the difference in having a wonderful and stress-free journey. This chapter will go over important topics to help you organize your vacation efficiently.

Choosing the Best Time to Visit

Langkawi's climate varies throughout the year, and the timing of your visit can significantly impact your experience. Here are some insights to help you decide the best time to explore this tropical paradise:

- Dry Season (November to March): This is considered the peak tourist season in Langkawi due to the pleasant weather, lower humidity, and minimal rainfall. If you prefer sunny days and outdoor activities, this is the ideal time to visit. Expect more significant crowds during this period, especially around December and January.

- Wet Season (April to October): While the wet season brings occasional heavy showers and higher humidity, Langkawi remains relatively warm and tropical even during this period. Hotel rates tend to be lower, and the island is less crowded, making it an excellent choice for budget-conscious travelers. Just be prepared for the occasional rainstorm.

- Shoulder Seasons (April, May, September, October): These months offer a balance between reasonable weather conditions and fewer crowds. It can be an excellent time to visit if you want to avoid the peak tourist season while still enjoying favorable weather.

Consider your preferences, budget, and willingness to cope with occasional rain when deciding on the best time for your Langkawi adventure.

Setting Your Budget

Langkawi offers a range of options to accommodate various budgets, making it accessible to both luxury seekers and budget-conscious travelers. Here's a breakdown of typical expenses:

- Accommodation: Prices for accommodation can vary significantly depending on the type and location. Here are some sample options:

  - Luxury: The Ritz-Carlton, Langkawi

- Contact: Website: www.ritzcarlton.com/langkawi
- Phone: +60 4-952 4888

- Mid-Range: Aseania Resort Langkawi
  - Contact: Website: www.aseanialangkawi.com
  - Phone: +60 4-955 2020

- Budget: Langkawi Dormitorio
  - Contact: Website: www.langkawidormitorio.com
  - Phone: +60 19-585 3007

- Food: Dining in Langkawi offers options for all budgets. Street food stalls and local restaurants offer affordable meals, while fine dining establishments can be more expensive.

- Transportation: Expenses will depend on your choice of transportation, but local buses and shared taxis are budget-friendly options.

- Activities: Langkawi offers a wide range of activities, from free nature walks to more expensive adventures like island hopping tours. Plan your activities based on your interests and budget.

- Miscellaneous: Don't forget to budget for souvenirs, entrance fees to attractions, and any additional expenses unique to your trip.

Setting a budget will help you plan your trip and ensure you have a comfortable and enjoyable experience on the island.

Accommodation Options

Langkawi offers a diverse range of accommodation options to suit various preferences and budgets. Here are a few sample accommodations along with their updated contact information:

1. The Ritz-Carlton, Langkawi

-

Website:www.ritzcarlton.com/langkawi

- Phone: +60 4-952 4888

- Description: A luxury beachfront resort offering stunning views, private beach access, spa facilities, and world-class dining.

2. Aseania Resort Langkawi

-Website: www.aseanialangkawi.com

- Phone: +60 4-955 2020

- Description: A mid-range resort with family-friendly amenities, including a swimming pool, water slides, and comfortable rooms.

3. Langkawi Dormitorio -
Website:www.langkawidormitorio.com

 - Phone: +60 19-585 3007

 - Description: A budget-friendly hostel offering dormitory-style accommodations for backpackers and budget travelers.

As you plan your trip, consider the location, facilities, and budget that align with your preferences. Booking in advance, especially during peak seasons, is recommended to secure your desired accommodation.

With these considerations in mind, you're well on your way to planning a memorable journey to Langkawi. In the chapters that follow, we will delve into the island's top attractions, activities, and dining options to ensure your Langkawi adventure is everything you dreamed it would be.

Creating an Itinerary

Langkawi's diverse attractions offer a wide array of experiences to suit every traveler's interests. Crafting a well-rounded itinerary ensures you make the most of your visit. Here's an exciting sample itinerary for a 5-day Langkawi adventure:

Day 1: Arrival and Sunset at Pantai Cenang

- Morning: Arrive at Langkawi International Airport and check in at your chosen accommodation.

- Afternoon: Relax on Pantai Cenang, one of the island's most popular beaches. Enjoy water sports, sunbathing, and beachfront dining.

- Evening: Watch a stunning sunset while sipping a cocktail at a beachside bar or restaurant.

Day 2: Island Hopping and Snorkeling

- Morning: Embark on an island-hopping tour that includes stops at Pulau Dayang Bunting, Pulau Singa Besar, and Pulau Beras Basah. Enjoy snorkeling, swimming, and exploring.

- Afternoon: Return to Langkawi and unwind at your accommodation.

- Evening: Explore Pantai Tengah's nightlife with dinner and live music at a beachfront venue.

Day 3: Mangrove Tour and Wildlife Encounters

- Morning: Join a mangrove tour through the Kilim Karst Geoforest Park. Witness incredible limestone formations, spot wildlife like eagles and monkeys, and explore the unique ecosystem.

- Afternoon: Visit the Langkawi Wildlife Park to get up close to exotic birds, reptiles, and mammals.
- Evening: Dine at a local seafood restaurant in Kuah Town.

Day 4: Sky Bridge and Cable Car Adventure
- Morning: Head to the Langkawi Cable Car and Sky Bridge. Enjoy panoramic views of the island from the cable car and walk on the breathtaking Sky Bridge.
- Afternoon: Visit Oriental Village for shopping and lunch.

- Evening: Return to Pantai Cenang for a relaxing evening by the beach.

Day 5: Nature and Culture Exploration
- Morning: Explore Telaga Tujuh Waterfall, also known as the Seven Wells Waterfall. Take a refreshing dip in its natural pools.

- Afternoon: Visit the Mahsuri Tomb and Cultural Complex to learn about Langkawi's history and the legend of Mahsuri.

- Evening: Enjoy a farewell dinner at a local Malay restaurant.

This itinerary offers a mix of natural beauty, adventure, cultural exploration, and relaxation, ensuring you experience the best of Langkawi in just five days. Feel free to adjust it based on your interests and the time you have available.

Travel Essentials and Packing Tips

Packing for Langkawi requires some careful consideration to ensure you're prepared for the tropical climate and the activities you plan to undertake. Here are some essential items and tips for your packing list:

1. Clothing:

 - Lightweight, breathable clothing like shorts, T-shirts, and dresses.

 - A swimsuit for beach days and water activities.

 - Comfortable walking shoes or sandals for exploring.

 - Light layers for cooler evenings during the dry season.

2. Sun Protection:

 - Sunscreen with high SPF.

 - Sunglasses and a wide-brimmed hat to shield from the sun.

 - Insect repellent for evening outings.

3. Travel Essentials:

 - Passport, visa (if required), and a photocopy of essential documents.

 - Travel insurance that covers medical emergencies.

- A power adapter for Malaysian plug types (Type G).

4. Medications and Toiletries:

- Any necessary prescription medications.

- Basic first-aid kit.

- Personal toiletries, including shampoo, conditioner, and sunscreen.

5. Electronics:

- Mobile phone and charger.

- Camera or smartphone for capturing memories.

- Power bank for on-the-go charging.

6. Miscellaneous:

- Reusable water bottle to stay hydrated.

- Cash or credit/debit cards for transactions (while many places accept cards, having some cash is advisable).

- A backpack or daypack for carrying essentials during outings.

Remember to pack light, and consider the specific requirements of your chosen activities, whether it's snorkeling gear, hiking shoes, or formal attire for fine dining. With these essentials and tips, you're ready to embark on your Langkawi adventure fully prepared and equipped for an unforgettable journey.

CHAPTER THREE: Exploring Langkawi's Neighborhoods

Langkawi's unique charm lies not only in its stunning natural beauty but also in its diverse neighborhoods, each offering its own distinct character and experiences. In this chapter, we'll take an in-depth look at Langkawi's top neighborhoods, including Pantai Cenang, Kuah Town, Datai Bay, and Telaga Harbor, to help you navigate the island and discover its hidden gems.

Pantai Cenang and the Beachfront

- Located on the western coast of Langkawi, Pantai Cenang is undoubtedly the island's most popular neighborhood, known for its vibrant beach scene and bustling atmosphere.

- The main attraction here is the stunning Pantai Cenang Beach, where you can soak up the sun, swim in the warm waters, and try water sports like jet-skiing and parasailing.

- Along the beachfront, you'll find a wide range of restaurants, bars, and shops, making it a lively hub for dining, nightlife, and souvenir shopping.

- Accommodation options in Pantai Cenang range from budget-friendly hostels to luxurious beachfront resorts, catering to all types of travelers.

Kuah Town and Shopping District

- Kuah Town, located on the southeastern side of Langkawi, serves as the island's commercial and transportation hub.

- This neighborhood is known for its duty-free shopping, making it a paradise for bargain hunters looking for alcohol, chocolates, cosmetics, and electronics.

- While Kuah Town doesn't have a beach, it offers cultural attractions like the Eagle Square with its impressive eagle sculpture and the Al-Hana Mosque.

- The town is also home to various seafood restaurants and local eateries where you can savor authentic Malay cuisine.

Datai Bay and Luxury Resorts

- Nestled on the northwestern coast, Datai Bay is a serene and upscale neighborhood known for its luxury resorts and pristine beaches.

- This area is renowned for The Datai Langkawi, a world-class resort known for its stunning rainforest setting, championship golf course, and access to Datai Beach.

- Datai Bay offers opportunities for golfing, spa treatments, and nature excursions, including guided rainforest walks and wildlife encounters.

- It's an ideal choice for travelers seeking a tranquil and luxurious retreat amidst Langkawi's natural beauty.

Telaga Harbor and the Marina

- Located on the western coast, Telaga Harbor is a vibrant waterfront neighborhood centered around the Telaga Harbor Park and Marina.

- This area is a hub for water-based activities, including yacht charters, island hopping tours, and sunset cruises.

- The Telaga Harbor Park is home to restaurants, cafes, boutiques, and even a cable car station that provides access to Langkawi's famous Sky Bridge.

- Visitors can stroll along the picturesque boardwalk, enjoy live music performances, and savor fresh seafood at waterfront restaurants.

Each of these neighborhoods offers a unique experience, from the bustling beachfront of Pantai

Cenang to the luxury and tranquility of Datai Bay. Depending on your interests and travel style, you can explore Langkawi's diverse neighborhoods and immerse yourself in the island's rich culture, natural beauty, and vibrant atmosphere. In the following sections of this guide, we'll delve deeper into the attractions, activities, and highlights of each neighborhood, helping you make the most of your Langkawi exploration.

CHAPTER FOUR:
Must-See Attractions

Langkawi is a treasure trove of natural and man-made wonders, and in this chapter, we'll delve into some of the island's most iconic and must-see attractions. From thrilling heights to captivating wildlife encounters, Langkawi promises a wide array of experiences for every type of traveler.

Langkawi Cable Car and Sky Bridge

Location: *Gunung Mat Cincang, Oriental Village, Burau Bay*

The Langkawi Cable Car and Sky Bridge are a dynamic duo of attractions that provide visitors with breathtaking views and heart-pounding excitement:

- Langkawi Cable Car: Start your journey at the Oriental Village and board the cable car, which will whisk you up the lush slopes of Gunung Mat Cincang. As you ascend, you'll be treated to panoramic vistas of the island's forests, cliffs, and the Andaman Sea.

- Sky Bridge: At the top station, don't miss the Langkawi Sky Bridge—a remarkable curved suspension bridge that offers vertigo-inducing views of the surrounding landscape. The Sky Bridge is particularly stunning during sunset, so time your visit accordingly.

- Tip: Arrive early to avoid crowds, especially during peak tourist seasons.

Langkawi Wildlife Park

Location: *Lot 1485, Jalan Ayer Hangat, Kampung Belanga Pecah*

For an up-close encounter with exotic wildlife, the Langkawi Wildlife Park is a must-visit:

- Flora and Fauna: Explore lush tropical gardens while marveling at a diverse range of animals, including birds, reptiles, and mammals. You can hand-feed parrots, watch crocodile feeding sessions, and interact with friendly rabbits.

- Educational: The park focuses on conservation and education, making it a great place for families and animal enthusiasts to learn about Langkawi's biodiversity.

- Photography: Don't forget your camera to capture memorable moments with colorful birds and other unique creatures.

Tanjung Rhu Beach

Location: *Tanjung Rhu, Langkawi*

Tanjung Rhu Beach is often hailed as one of Langkawi's most picturesque and tranquil spots:

- Natural Beauty: This beach is renowned for its pristine white sands and crystal-clear waters. It's an ideal place for sunbathing, leisurely walks, and enjoying the serenity of nature.

- Mangrove Tours: Nearby, you can embark on mangrove boat tours to explore the intricate ecosystems of Kilim Karst Geoforest Park.
- Luxury Resorts: Tanjung Rhu is also home to upscale resorts that offer fine dining and spa experiences.

Langkawi Underwater World

Location: *Pantai Cenang, Langkawi*

For a journey beneath the waves without getting wet, Langkawi Underwater World is a top choice:

- Aquatic Wonderland: This aquarium houses an impressive array of marine life, including sharks, rays, penguins, and colorful coral reef exhibits.

- Interactive Experiences: Visitors can enjoy hands-on experiences such as feeding sessions with fish and turtles.

- Educational: The aquarium is educational for all ages, making it an excellent family-friendly attraction.

Langkawi Geopark

Location: *Kilim Karst Geoforest Park, Langkawi*

A UNESCO-listed geopark, Langkawi's geological wonders are a testament to the island's ancient history:

- Mangrove Cruises: Explore the intricate mangrove forests, limestone formations, and hidden caves on guided boat tours.

- Fossilized Forest: Discover the intriguing fossilized sea creatures preserved in the limestone rocks.

- Eagle Watching: Kilim Karst Geoforest Park is also home to a thriving population of eagles, including the majestic Brahminy kites.

Eagle Square (Dataran Lang)

Location: *Kuah Town, Langkawi*

Eagle Square is an iconic symbol of Langkawi, featuring a massive sculpture of an eagle poised for flight:

- Landmark: The square is a popular gathering spot and serves as the entrance to Kuah Jetty.

- Views: Enjoy scenic views of the sea and nearby islands, making it an ideal location for photos.

- Night Illumination: The eagle sculpture is illuminated at night, creating a stunning visual spectacle.

These must-see attractions offer a glimpse into the diverse experiences awaiting you on the island of Langkawi. Whether you're seeking adventure, relaxation, or an educational journey, Langkawi has something to captivate every traveler's heart.

CHAPTER FIVE: Experiencing Langkawi's Culture

Langkawi's culture is a vibrant tapestry woven from its Malay heritage, diverse influences, and the warm hospitality of its people. In this chapter, we'll delve into the island's cultural aspects, from its culinary delights to traditional arts and crafts.

Langkawi's Culinary Scene

Langkawi's culinary scene is a delightful fusion of flavors influenced by Malay, Thai, Chinese, and Indian cuisines. Here are some culinary experiences you shouldn't miss:

1. Seafood Delights: As an island, Langkawi boasts a bounty of fresh seafood. Savor dishes like grilled fish, prawns, and squid at local seafood restaurants along Pantai Cenang and Pantai Kok.

2. Nasi Campur: This Malay dish offers a colorful array of flavors and textures, featuring rice served with various side dishes, such as rendang (spicy beef), sambal (chili paste), and fried fish.

3. Roti Canai: A popular breakfast or snack option, roti canai is a type of flatbread served with dhal (lentil curry) or chicken curry. You'll find it at local eateries throughout Langkawi.

4. Tropical Fruits: Langkawi is known for its abundance of tropical fruits, including rambutan, durian, and mango. Try them fresh or as part of fruit salads and desserts.

Traditional Malay Cuisine

Exploring traditional Malay cuisine is an essential part of experiencing Langkawi's culture:

1. Nasi Lemak: Considered Malaysia's national dish, nasi lemak is a fragrant rice dish cooked in coconut milk, served with sambal, anchovies, peanuts, and a boiled or fried egg.

2. Satay: Skewers of marinated and grilled meat (usually chicken, beef, or lamb) served with peanut sauce and a side of rice cakes or cucumber-onion salad.

3. Rendang: A rich and flavorful dry curry dish made with tender meat, coconut milk, and a blend of aromatic spices.

4. Teh Tarik: Malaysia's national drink, teh tarik is a strong and creamy pulled tea that's a favorite among locals.

Festivals and Events

Langkawi hosts various festivals and events throughout the year, providing opportunities to immerse yourself in local traditions:

1. Langkawi International Maritime and Aerospace Exhibition (LIMA): Held biennially, LIMA is one of Asia's premier aerospace and maritime events, featuring impressive airshows and maritime displays.

2. Langkawi Arts in Paradise Festival: Celebrating local and international arts, this festival showcases exhibitions, performances, and workshops by artists from various disciplines.

3. Harvest Festival (Pesta Lada): A celebration of the rice harvest, this festival features traditional dance performances, sports events, and cultural exhibitions.

Traditional Arts and Crafts

Langkawi is a hub for traditional arts and crafts, and you can explore the island's rich heritage through these activities:

1. Batik Painting: Engage in a batik painting workshop to create your own colorful fabric art piece using the traditional wax-resist dyeing technique.

2. Pandak Beach T-shirt Painting: Visit Pantai Cenang's Pandak Beach to paint your custom T-shirt, a popular and artistic souvenir.

3. Songket Weaving: Discover the intricate art of weaving songket, a traditional Malay fabric known for its beautiful patterns and designs.

Local Markets and Souvenirs

Exploring local markets is a fantastic way to immerse yourself in Langkawi's culture and take home unique souvenirs:

1. Langkawi Night Market: Held in various locations around the island, this nightly market offers a diverse array of street food, clothing, accessories, and handicrafts.

2. Cenang Street Market: Located in Pantai Cenang, this market is known for its handmade jewelry, clothing, and local snacks.

3. Ayer Hangat Friday Night Market: Experience the lively atmosphere of this weekly market, featuring delicious street food and a wide selection of local products.

Whether you're sampling the flavors of traditional Malay cuisine, participating in local festivals, or hunting for unique souvenirs in bustling markets, Langkawi's culture is a treasure waiting to be discovered. Embrace the island's rich heritage, and your Langkawi adventure will be enriched with memorable experiences and a deeper connection to the local way of life.

CHAPTER SIX:
Outdoor Adventures and Recreation

Langkawi's natural beauty is a playground for outdoor enthusiasts, offering a plethora of activities that allow you to immerse yourself in the island's breathtaking landscapes. From the shores to the rainforests, here are some of the most exciting outdoor adventures and recreation options in Langkawi:

Beach Activities and Water Sports

Langkawi's pristine beaches provide the perfect backdrop for a variety of beach activities and water sports:

1. Swimming and Sunbathing: The island's beaches, like Pantai Cenang and Pantai Tengah, offer ideal conditions for swimming and sunbathing. Unwind on the soft sands and cool off in the azure waters.

2. Water Sports: Thrill-seekers can indulge in water sports such as jet-skiing, parasailing, banana boat rides, and windsurfing. Rental facilities are widely available on popular beaches.

3. Snorkeling and Diving: Langkawi's clear waters are home to diverse marine life and coral reefs. Take a snorkeling or diving trip to explore the underwater wonders, including colorful fish and vibrant coral gardens.

Trekking in Langkawi's Rainforests

Langkawi's lush rainforests are a haven for hikers and nature enthusiasts:

1. Langkawi Wildlife Park and Jungle Trails: Combine a visit to the Langkawi Wildlife Park with nearby jungle trails like the Sungai Kilim Nature Park for a day of birdwatching, wildlife spotting, and hiking.

2. Gunung Mat Cincang: Ascend this majestic mountain for a challenging trek. The trail rewards hikers with panoramic views from the summit and access to the Langkawi Cable Car.

3. Seven Wells Waterfall: Hike to the Seven Wells Waterfall, a series of cascading pools surrounded by verdant rainforest. The hike involves steep staircases but is well worth the effort.

Island Hopping and Boat Tours

Exploring the nearby islands and geological wonders is a must during your Langkawi adventure:

1. Island Hopping: Join an island-hopping tour that includes stops at nearby islets like Pulau Dayang Bunting, Pulau Singa Besar, and Pulau Beras Basah. Enjoy swimming, snorkeling, and beachcombing.

2. Mangrove Tours: Discover the intricate ecosystems of Langkawi's mangrove forests on guided boat tours through Kilim Karst Geoforest Park. Look out for eagles, monkeys, and limestone formations.

Golfing in Langkawi

Langkawi offers golfers an opportunity to enjoy the sport against a stunning backdrop:

1. The Els Club Teluk Datai: Designed by legendary golfer Ernie Els, this 18-hole championship golf course is nestled within a lush rainforest, providing a challenging and scenic golfing experience.

Day Trips and Excursions

Explore the surrounding islands and attractions on day trips and excursions:

1. Pulau Payar Marine Park: Take a day trip to Pulau Payar, Langkawi's premier marine park. Snorkel, dive, or simply relax on the pristine beach.

2. Koh Lipe, Thailand: Consider a day trip to the nearby Thai island of Koh Lipe, known for its crystal-clear waters, vibrant coral reefs, and laid-back atmosphere. Ensure you have the necessary travel documents, such as a visa, for entry into Thailand.

Langkawi's outdoor adventures and recreation options cater to travelers of all interests and activity levels. Whether you're seeking adrenaline-pumping water sports, peaceful nature hikes, or leisurely boat tours, the island's natural wonders provide a playground for unforgettable experiences in the great outdoors.

CHAPTER SEVEN:
Langkawi for Families, Seniors, and Solo Travelers

Langkawi is a versatile destination that caters to a wide range of travelers, including families, seniors, and solo adventurers. In this chapter, we'll explore the various ways Langkawi welcomes and accommodates each of these groups.

Family-Friendly Activities

Langkawi's family-friendly atmosphere and diverse range of activities make it an excellent choice for travelers with children:

1. Langkawi Wildlife Park: A visit to the Langkawi Wildlife Park allows kids to get up close and personal

with exotic birds, reptiles, and mammals. Feeding sessions and interactive experiences make it an educational and entertaining stop.

2. Underwater World Langkawi: This aquarium is a hit with kids. They can marvel at the marine life on display, walk through the underwater tunnel, and even participate in feeding sessions.

3. Pantai Cenang Beach: The island's most popular beach offers gentle waves and a family-friendly atmosphere. Kids can play in the sand, swim, and enjoy ice cream from beachfront vendors.

4. Island Hopping Tours: Family-friendly island hopping tours are a great way to explore nearby islets and enjoy activities like snorkeling, swimming, and picnicking on secluded beaches.

5. Kilim Karst Geoforest Park: Take a mangrove boat tour through this geopark, where kids can spot wildlife, including eagles and monkeys, and marvel at the unique limestone formations.

Langkawi for Seniors

Langkawi's tranquil ambiance and accessibility make it an ideal destination for seniors looking for relaxation and exploration:

1. Nature Walks: Seniors can enjoy leisurely nature walks in the rainforest, exploring attractions like Telaga Tujuh Waterfall and the Langkawi Cable Car.

2. Cultural Experiences: Visit cultural sites like the Mahsuri Tomb and Cultural Complex in Kuah Town to learn about Langkawi's history and folklore.

3. Island Hopping: Consider taking a relaxed island hopping tour with comfortable boat transfers and opportunities for sightseeing.

4. Beachfront Relaxation: Many resorts in Langkawi offer beachfront accommodations, providing a serene environment for relaxation.

5. Golf: Golf enthusiasts can tee off at The Els Club Teluk Datai, which offers a picturesque course amidst the rainforest.

Solo Travel Tips and Safety

Langkawi is a safe and welcoming destination for solo travelers. Here are some tips to enhance your solo adventure:

1. Accommodation: Choose well-reviewed accommodations with positive guest feedback and consider staying in social hostels or guesthouses to meet fellow travelers.

2. Local Transportation: Use reliable and registered transportation services, such as taxis, to get around the island. Ride-sharing apps may also be available.

3. Exploration: Langkawi is relatively safe to explore on your own. However, always inform someone about your plans and estimated return time when embarking on outdoor adventures.

4. Safety Precautions: Take standard safety precautions, such as safeguarding your belongings and staying hydrated during outdoor activities.

5. Meeting Locals and Fellow Travelers: Join local tours and excursions to meet both locals and fellow travelers. Engaging in activities like cooking classes or group tours can be an excellent way to make new friends.

Meeting Locals and Making Friends

Connecting with locals can enrich your Langkawi experience and provide a deeper understanding of the island's culture:

1. Local Markets: Visit local markets like the Langkawi Night Market to interact with vendors and sample authentic Malaysian street food.

2. Joining Activities: Participate in local activities such as fishing trips, traditional dance classes, or batik workshops, which often involve interaction with locals.

3. Cultural Festivals: Attend cultural festivals and events to engage with the local community and enjoy traditional performances and celebrations.

4. Volunteering: Consider volunteering with local organizations or wildlife conservation efforts if you plan to stay for an extended period.

5. Language: Learning a few basic Malay phrases can go a long way in breaking the ice and building connections with locals.

Langkawi's warm and welcoming community makes it easy to forge connections and create lasting memories, whether you're traveling with family, enjoying a peaceful retirement, or embarking on a solo adventure.

CHAPTER EIGHT:
Practical Information and
Resources

As you prepare for your Langkawi adventure, it's essential to have practical information and resources at your fingertips to ensure a smooth and enjoyable trip. In this chapter, we'll cover important topics such as money and currency, language and communication, safety, and health tips to help you plan and stay informed.

Money and Currency

1. Currency: The currency used in Langkawi is the Malaysian Ringgit (MYR), often abbreviated as RM. It's advisable to exchange some currency before arriving or withdraw cash from ATMs on the island.

2. ATMs: ATM machines are widely available throughout Langkawi, particularly in major towns like Pantai Cenang and Kuah Town. International credit and debit cards are accepted at most hotels, restaurants, and larger businesses.

3. Currency Exchange: You can exchange foreign currency at banks, currency exchange offices, and some hotels. Rates may vary, so it's a good idea to compare rates before exchanging money.

4. Tipping: Tipping is not mandatory in Malaysia, but it is appreciated for good service. In restaurants, a service charge is sometimes included in the bill. If it's not, a tip of 10% is customary.

Language and Communication

1. Language: The official language of Malaysia is Malay (Bahasa Malaysia), but English is widely spoken, especially in the tourism industry. Many signs, menus, and information are available in both Malay and English.

2. Communication: Mobile phone coverage is generally reliable in Langkawi, with good network connectivity. International roaming services may apply, so check with your provider for rates and plans. Local SIM cards can be purchased for data and local calls.

3. Internet: Most hotels, cafes, and restaurants offer free Wi-Fi to customers. If you need constant access, consider purchasing a local SIM card with data.

Safety and Health Tips

1. Safety: Langkawi is a safe destination for travelers. However, as with any travel, exercise common sense and take precautions:

   - Keep your belongings secure in crowded areas.

   - Use registered transportation services.

   - Respect local customs and laws, such as dress codes in religious sites.

2. Health Precautions:

   - Ensure your vaccinations are up-to-date before traveling.

   - Drink bottled or purified water to avoid stomach issues.

   - Apply sunscreen and wear a hat to protect yourself from the sun's strong rays.

   - Use insect repellent in areas with mosquitos.

- Consider travel insurance that covers medical emergencies.

3. Medical Facilities: Langkawi has medical facilities and clinics, including Langkawi Hospital in Kuah Town. It's advisable to have travel insurance that covers medical emergencies.

4. Emergency Numbers: In case of emergency, dial the following numbers:
   - Police: 999
   - Fire and Rescue: 994
   - Ambulance: 999

5. Local Customs: Respect local customs, particularly in religious sites. Modest clothing is recommended when visiting temples and mosques.

6. Environmental Responsibility: Protect Langkawi's fragile ecosystem by following Leave No Trace principles. Dispose of trash responsibly and avoid damaging coral reefs and marine life during water activities.

7. Travel Advisory: Check for any travel advisories or updates from your country's embassy or consulate before and during your trip.

By staying informed and prepared with practical information and resources, you can enjoy your Langkawi journey with confidence and peace of mind, knowing you have the tools and knowledge to navigate the island safely and responsibly.

Sustainable Travel in Langkawi

Sustainable travel practices are essential for preserving the natural beauty and cultural heritage of Langkawi. Here are some tips to help you travel responsibly and minimize your environmental impact:

1. Respect the Environment: Take care of Langkawi's stunning natural landscapes by adhering to Leave No Trace principles. Avoid littering, stay on marked trails, and do not disturb wildlife.

2. Reduce Plastic Use: Bring a reusable water bottle and shopping bag to minimize plastic waste. Refill your bottle at hotels and restaurants that offer purified water stations.

3. Choose Eco-Friendly Tours: Support tour operators and activities that prioritize eco-friendly practices, such

as responsible wildlife encounters and sustainable boating tours.

4. Conserve Energy and Water: Be mindful of energy and water consumption by turning off lights, air conditioning, and taps when not in use. Many accommodations have sustainability initiatives in place.

5. Support Local Communities: Purchase souvenirs and products made by local artisans to support the livelihoods of local communities. Visit local markets and eateries to engage with residents and contribute to the local economy.

Useful Contacts and Emergency Numbers

During your stay in Langkawi, it's helpful to have important contact information readily available. Here are some updated contact numbers for essential services:

1. Emergency Services:
   - Police: 999
   - Fire and Rescue: 994
   - Ambulance: 999

2. Langkawi International Airport:
   - Phone: +604-955 1311

3. Langkawi Tourist Information Center (Kedah Tourism):
   - Phone: +604-966 7789

4. Langkawi Hospital:
   - Phone: +604-508 4888

5. Tourist Police:

  - Phone: +604-966 3523

6. Consulates and Embassies (for international travelers): In case of emergencies or lost passports, contact your country's nearest consulate or embassy in Malaysia.

7. Local Transportation Services:

  - Langkawi Taxi Association: +604-955 1311

  - Langkawi Grab (Ride-Sharing): Available through the Grab app

8. Travel Insurance Provider: Save the contact information for your travel insurance provider, including their emergency helpline.

Remember to keep these contact numbers accessible but secure, such as in your phone's contacts or written down in a travel journal. While Langkawi is a safe destination, being prepared with emergency numbers and essential contacts can provide peace of mind during your visit.

APPENDIX I:
Useful Travel Resources

As you embark on your Langkawi adventure, having access to helpful travel resources can greatly enhance your experience. Here are some valuable resources, including travel apps, a Langkawi travel checklist, and currency and banking information:

Helpful Travel Apps

1. Google Maps: An invaluable tool for navigation, finding local attractions, and locating nearby restaurants and services.

2. Grab: If you need transportation within Langkawi, Grab is a convenient ride-sharing app widely used in Southeast Asia.

3. XE Currency Converter: Easily convert currencies and stay updated on exchange rates for your trip.

4. Weather Apps: Install a weather app to check Langkawi's weather forecast and plan your outdoor activities accordingly.

5. TripAdvisor: Access reviews, recommendations, and traveler insights on Langkawi's attractions, accommodations, and restaurants.

6. XE Travel Expense Calculator: Helps you keep track of your travel expenses and currency conversions.

7. Language Apps: Download language translation apps or phrasebooks to assist with communication in Malay, the local language.

Langkawi Travel Check

Before you depart for Langkawi, use this checklist to ensure you have everything in order for a smooth journey:

- Travel Documents:
    - Passport (with at least six months validity)
    - Visa (if required)
    - Flight tickets and itinerary
    - Hotel reservations

- Health and Safety:
    - Travel insurance policy and contact information
    - Necessary vaccinations and medications
    - First aid kit

- Finances:
    - Sufficient local currency (Malaysian Ringgit)

- Debit/credit cards

- Traveler's checks (if preferred)

- Electronics and Communication:

  - Mobile phone with charger and travel adapter

  - Power bank

    - Copies of important documents (passport, ID, insurance)

- Travel Gear:

  - Suitable clothing for the climate

    - Comfortable shoes for walking and outdoor activities

  - Sunscreen, sunglasses, and a hat

  - Travel backpack or daypack

- Extras:

  - Travel guidebook or printed itinerary

  - Travel pillow and eye mask for long flights

- Snacks and a reusable water bottle

Currency and Banking Information

1. Currency: The currency used in Langkawi is the Malaysian Ringgit (MYR), often abbreviated as RM.

2. ATMs: ATMs are readily available throughout Langkawi, particularly in major towns like Pantai Cenang and Kuah Town. International credit and debit cards are widely accepted.

3. Currency Exchange: Exchange foreign currency at banks, currency exchange offices, and some hotels. Rates may vary, so it's a good idea to compare rates before exchanging money.

4. Tipping: Tipping is not mandatory in Malaysia, but it is appreciated for good service. In restaurants, a

service charge is sometimes included in the bill. If it's not, a tip of 10% is customary.

Having these resources at your disposal will help you stay organized and informed throughout your Langkawi journey, ensuring you make the most of your time on this beautiful island.

APPENDIX II:
Glossary of Malay Phrases

While English is widely spoken in Langkawi, learning a few basic Malay phrases can enhance your travel experience and help you communicate with locals. Here's a glossary of Malay phrases categorized into common scenarios for travelers:

Basic Phrases for Travelers

1. Hello: Selamat pagi (morning), Selamat tengah hari (midday), Selamat petang (afternoon/evening)

2. Thank you: Terima kasih

3. Please: Sila

4. Yes: Ya

5. No: Tidak

6. Excuse me / Sorry: Maaf

7. How much is this?: Berapa harganya?

8. Where is...?: Di mana...

9. I need help: Saya perlukan bantuan

10. Goodbye: Selamat tinggal

Ordering Food and Drinks

1. Menu: Menu

2. Water: Air

3. Food: Makanan

4. Rice: Nasi

5. Noodles: Mee

6. Chicken: Ayam

7. Beef: Daging lembu

8. Fish: Ikan

9. Vegetables: Sayur-sayuran

10. Spicy: Pedas

11. Mild: Tidak pedas

12. Coffee: Kopi

13. Tea: Teh

14. Milk: Susu

15. Sugar: Gula

Navigating Public Transportation

1. Bus: Bas

2. Taxi: Teksi

3. Train: Kereta api

4. Ticket: Tiket

5. Station: Stesen

6. Airport: Lapangan terbang

7. Boat: Bot

8. Ferry: Feri

9. Port: Pelabuhan

10. Bus Stop: Hentian bas

11. Train Station: Stesen kereta api

12. Airport Terminal: Terminal lapangan terbang

13. How much is a ticket to...?: Berapa harga tiket ke...?

14. Where is the bus/train station?: Di mana stesen bas/kereta api?

15. I need to go to...: Saya perlu pergi ke...

These Malay phrases can be a helpful tool for bridging the language gap and showing respect for the local culture. While many locals in Langkawi speak English, making an effort to use these phrases can lead to more meaningful interactions and a richer travel experience.

APPENDIX III:

Maps of Langkawi

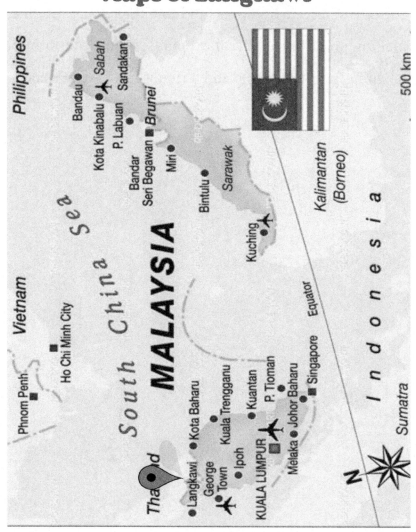

Printed in Great Britain
by Amazon

30840058R00056